What I Didn't Learn in Real Estate School*

Ann Taddeo

with Phil Smith

And Not Just About Real Estate

Copyright © 2018 by Ann Taddeo

All rights reserved

ISBN 9781724995155

Printed in the United States

This book is dedicated to my husband, Anthony Taddeo, my sons Patrick and Paul, and my daughter, Faith. They've been with me always, through times good and bad, and they are responsible as much as I am for whatever success I've enjoyed. It is theirs as well as mine.

Contents

Chapter 1	Birth of a Future Realtor	7
Chapter 2	My Real Estate Career Begins	11
Chapter 3	I Start My Own Company	17
Chapter 4	For First-Time Buyers	21
Chapter 5	What I Do for My Clients	29
Chapter 6	What I Need From My Clients	47
Chapter 7	Real Estate Business Models	57
Chapter 8	Stories, I Have Stories	63
Chapter 9	Networking and Connecting	71
Chapter 10	What I've Learned About Life	81

Chapter 1

Birth of a Future Realtor

Looking back at my childhood, I can see I was destined to become a Realtor.

Whether at work or at play, I was always negotiating. I was a natural at it.

Born on May 23, 1965, I grew up in Thornton, Colo., a northern suburb of Denver, as an only child in the 1980s. My parents are Ed and Vivian Gardner.

Throughout junior high and high school, my friend Michelle (Mickey) and I were always together. This was before video games, smartphones and computers, and we loved to play board games: Yahtzee, Risk, and especially Monopoly. We'd play Monopoly for hours, sometimes even taking a break to go to sleep only to resume the game in the morning.

Here's where the negotiating came in: We didn't believe in buying, selling and trading the properties for what the deed specified. We'd always bargain hard with each other, and whoever was in the best position overall in the game would usually win that round of negotiations.

The fact that we were friends didn't have anything to do with it.

Each one of us did our best to get the best of the other, knowing that was the way to win the game. Getting enough funny money together to put up those green homes and red hotels all around the board gave me a little rush of adrenaline.

It's not totally like being in real estate for real, of course. In the real world, a negotiation over a home or a property ideally ends with both parties being happy. But we were teenage girls, and the name of the game was ruthlessness.

She kicked my butt in Risk, the game of world domination. She was more ruthless than me in that game, and it used to make me mad. At Monopoly it was more even and I held my own.

We used to babysit for the same families, and whenever one of us was working somewhere, the other would usually show up.

I started babysitting when I was 13, my first job. (I've hardly ever been without a job since then; sometimes more than one).

Babysitting wasn't a natural job for me because I'm not all that fond of kids (unless they're super-cute!). When somebody brings a baby around and everybody's going weepy and google-eyed, that's not me. I don't need to smell the baby and I don't need to hold the baby.

But even babysitting gave me some valuable lessons in negotiating and human nature. Kids can be pretty conniving and I had to learn how to deal with it.

Their parents would usually give them a specific bedtime. The kids, of course, didn't want to go to bed when they were supposed to. They'd somehow manage to stretch it to 15 minutes past 9, or whenever they were supposed to hit the sack, and 15 minutes later they'd have to get up and go to the bathroom, and 15 minutes after that they'd want a glass of water.

So I got smart and started making them do all that before they went to bed. I'd even give them a little leeway if they behaved. A lot of times the parents said not to do that, and to enforce bedtime strictly. But I figured maybe letting them stay up a little later was fairly harmless. At any rate, it made the time go a little more smoothly.

The babysitting experience helped me learn a little bit of patience, and the kids' conniving nature showed me a thing or two about getting along in the business world. (Not that some adults act like kids–except that they do!)

This bit of insight into human nature has served me well in my real estate career. When you're negotiating, or even working with clients whose interests are theoretically the same as yours, it helps to have an understanding of what motivates people, what type of treatment they'll respond to, and how to make them see where their interests truly lie. You have to treat different people different ways, and I first learned that at age 13.

A year later, I started working at a pizza place near my home. I waited tables and took phone orders. There I got my first glimpse of the nasty underbelly of American business.

The owner was a pervert, and I got sick of his constant innuendos and the creepy vibes he put out. But somehow I lasted a year there.

At age 16 I went to work at a KFC restaurant (it was Kentucky Fried Chicken then; the word "fried" didn't have the same negative connotations that it has now). This turned out to be a much better experience for me. The manager liked me and I liked him, and when he moved to another store he took me with him to be the assistant manager.

At age 19, I got to manage my own KFC store. I was working 30 hours a week there while going to college.

I was a sophomore at Metro State in downtown Denver, and I've since learned that in your second year of college it's typical to ask if that's what you really want to do. That's what I went through, and ultimately I decided I was done with school. So I dropped out of Metro, moved out on my own and managed the KFC restaurant for a year.

I also helped open a B. Dalton book store. B. Dalton was a chain that went out of business in 2010, like so many companies the victim of amazon.com and the Internet revolution. Ironically, B. Dalton, along with Borders and Barnes & Noble, had earlier put hundreds if not thousands of independent bookstores out of business.

I got married shortly thereafter and quit my jobs to serve as the full-time secretary for my father-in-law's water well company.

My life changed again in October 1988 when I was 23. I delivered my first child, Patrick O'Brien, and two years later had my second son, Paul. Even though I wasn't super kid-friendly, I started a day care business in my home. It was a way to keep on working while I was bringing up my boys.

But I got out of that after a 10-year-old kid and his stepbrother started telling lies about me. A social worker even came by and cleared me of any wrongdoing, but the whole experience soured me on running a day care facility.

I was about to find the career I was meant to be in, the career that all those Monopoly games I played as a girl foreshadowed.

But it took a couple of kicks in the pants to finally get me there.

Chapter 2
My Real Estate Career Begins

My first husband and I–and thank the Lord we're exes now!–had some bad experiences with real estate agents, and that's what eventually led to my own real estate career.

In the early 1990s, we were looking to buy a house. At the time, interest rates were high and a lot of people were taking out adjustable-rate mortgages (ARMs) to save a few interest points. We didn't want to, but the agent we were working with kept pushing us to take an adjustable loan so we could buy more house (and more critically to her, she could get a bigger commission). She even asked us to borrow money from my parents, which we didn't have any intention of doing.

Not only that, but she made me feel stupid. I asked her about points (which I now understand to be a percentage of the mortgage amount you can choose to pay up front to get a better interest rate), and she couldn't or wouldn't explain it so that I could understand. It was very uncomfortable, but we ended up buying a home from her anyway.

After this experience, it dawned on me that there's no such thing as a stupid question. That lesson has always stuck with me, and as I'm working with clients and they don't understand the way I explain something, I explain it a different way and keep on trying until they understand. I'm fully aware that some situations in real estate can be difficult and hard to grasp if you're not in that world.

A few years after that, we got a call from an agent asking if we wanted to sell our house and buy another. We said sure.

So we went out house-hunting with him on weekends. Back then of course there was no Internet, so the only way to find a house for sale was to drive around looking for signs or enlist a real estate agent. We went around with him on weekends looking at houses. But he couldn't find us anything right away, and he dropped us like we were radioactive. He said he'd set us up with another agent, but never did.

I felt ditched.

But this agent did have one positive effect on my life. He said I should consider going into real estate. He must have sensed something about me that even I hadn't known.

I thought about it. I wondered if I could do it. And thankfully, I decided I should give it a shot.

It was 1994 and the market was good. (It isn't always, as I was to find out several times over the next 20-plus years.) I went to real estate school two nights a week.

It made me realize it was going to be tougher than I thought.

And school didn't really teach me a single thing about how to be a successful real estate agent. What it did do was give me just enough to pass the test, including contracts, settlement sheets, the rudiments of real estate law, how to measure a property, eminent domain and so on.

Nothing about marketing, nothing about dealing with different demographics, nothing about building rapport with people, very little about negotiating, and nothing about the psychology involved in the business.

For instance, how do you explain to sellers that just because they need $200,000 for their house, that doesn't mean it's worth $200,000.

That's the kind of thing that just comes with experience.

I passed the test, though it took three times, and became a licensed real estate agent.

(I had the material down cold; it's just that I have text anxiety and the first two times I barely missed passing.)

When I finally got a passing grade I hugged the proctor and told him I was glad I'd never have to see him again!

I didn't become a Realtor until I joined the National Association of Realtors, which owns the title along with the Canadian Real Estate Association. Most people think the term Realtor applies to any licensed agent; it doesn't.

However, I realized immediately that I didn't know anything. As in most fields of endeavor, you know nothing about operating a real estate practice until you've been out there doing it.

Still, it didn't take me long to discover that I had found my true passion in life. Being a Realtor, and finding some early success, gave me a real sense of independence and self-esteem. I hadn't had much of the latter because my then-husband was emotionally abusive and only supportive of me to the extent that I brought home the money.

I began my career at Century 21, one of a number of nationally franchised real estate operations (others include Coldwell Banker, Keller Williams and RE/MAX).

I was grateful that Century 21 hired me, because few real estate offices were taking on newcomers at the time.

With the market going so strong, I was able to start making a living right away. In one month's time within the first year, I closed eight transactions. I thought I was going to die!

Nonetheless, some more experienced agents and customers treated me with little respect. It used to make me mad when they asked me how long I'd been licensed, maybe because of my lingering lack of self-esteem. Those experiences have caused me to do whatever I can to help newer agents I'm dealing with now.

As the office newbie, I had to cold-call, do floor duty, knock on people's doors, put up flags in people's yards on the 4th of July and tasks like that.

When I say floor duty, I mean being in the office to answer the phone, greet people who walk in and help them out if they don't have a specific agent in mind. I can remember being on the floor and listening to everybody's horror stories, mostly about deals that fell apart. I absorbed everything. It made me realize even more how much I had to learn.

My mentor at Century 21 was my office manager, Mary Morse. She was really hard on me but she made me think. She spent a lot of time with me, which was important because she seemed to know the instant somebody walked in the door if they were going to make it in the business. If her judgment was that they wouldn't, she wouldn't go out of her way for them. Like the previous agent who suggested I should go into real estate, Mary saw something in me.

She spent a lot of time going over different scenarios with me. What should we do in this situation? What would happen if we did that?

Mary was an interesting person. She was in her mid-50s and had short, dark brown hair. She smoked like a frickin' train. We had one room in the office that was for smokers and her desk was in the back of the room.

To go see her you practically had to separate the smoke with your hands.

Yes, she was hard on me, but it was all for my own good and she was always willing to help me. She's still in real estate and we're Facebook friends. I have a lot of respect for her.

I wish I could remember my first deal, but the details have escaped me.

I do know that for every deal I closed at Century 21, I paid part of my commission to the broker who owned the office.

This was standard practice at the time, but since then many real estate companies have changed their structure so that agents pay a monthly fee to the owner, not a commission split.

After two years at Century 21, I got my broker's license (previously I had had only an agent's license) in 1996 and took my license to Metro Brokers. A regional company based in Denver, this was one of the 100 percent commission companies that were then springing up.

This was a whole new ballgame for me. At Century 21, if I didn't do any business I didn't owe the broker anything. But now with Metro Brokers, the bill came due every month whether I closed any transactions or not.

My first transaction with Metro Brokers turned out to be a nightmare. It involved a young couple who were buying a house, and it was supposed to close on Monday. On the previous Friday afternoon, the sellers were packing their belongings. I got a call from the couple and they were getting a divorce. The deal fell through.

I was pretty devastated, but it wasn't long before I got another deal. And I was on my way to a richly rewarding career that I couldn't have envisioned even two years earlier.

I was still working for my in-laws' company during my early years in real estate. But that all changed in July 1999. After putting up with my husband's abuse for 13 years, enough was enough. When I was done I was done. I left him and we were divorced on Feb. 11, 2000.

That was my liberation day! And just a year later, I took another plunge and started my own company, American Dream Realty.

Chapter 3
I Start My Own Company

At the beginning of 2000, I freed myself from my mentally abusive husband.

A year later, having done fairly well in the real estate business working for another brokerage, I decided to form my own company.

It wasn't an easy decision. But it followed naturally from everything I had accomplished.

What actually precipitated the move was that I had been hanging my license at a Metro Brokers office in Northglenn, a northern Denver suburb that's west of my home in Brighton.

But I basically worked from home and hardly ever went to the office. I tried to get on with the Metro Brokers office in Brighton, but they weren't taking agents who worked from home.

After thinking about it, I realized that even while under the Metro Brokers umbrella, I had pretty much been on my own. I was paying a "desk fee," and I didn't even have a desk at the brokerage. So why should I keep giving up that money every month? The way I figured it, my only option was to go out on my own.

So I just did it.

I was still feeling somewhat beat down from my marriage, but I was gaining some fragile self-confidence and making friends. I was on my own–well, on my own with my two sons–and living a life I had never lived before.

The first thing I had to decide on was a name for my company. That was critically important. One day I had an epiphany: What is homeownership but realizing the American dream? I wanted something that expressed to people how I feel about helping them find their dream home. So I tentatively decided on American Dream Realty. Naturally, I chose red, white and blue as my primary colors.

I searched the Colorado Secretary of State's website and found there was no company in the state with that name. I registered as an LLC (limited liability company) and I was off.

I later found out that there was a company called American Dream Home Realty, but I never had any problem with them. And that company no longer exists.

I didn't have a lot of money to spend, so I had my son Patrick design my logo, a simple drawing of a house. I used it for 15 years, until I had a new one designed by a professional. I must admit that it was very hard to make the change, but I had to keep my logo current and updated.

Some of the things I did to save money back then were, shall we say, creative. I had a friend with a big printer and she could produce vinyl signs. So I sent her a workup for my yard sign, she made them and I stuck them over my old signs. That got me by until I could afford to buy new signs.

I don't remember feeling too much stress. I always knew I would make it. When you're doing something like that, you're so starry-eyed that you don't see it as an option to fail.

I had to fight hard because I was the little guy; not part of a franchise operation, not even part of a small local or regional company.

Actually, I was able to turn that to my benefit. Some real estate companies pressure their agents to favor listings from other agents from the same company. I didn't have to deal with that. I could deal with any agents from anywhere.

At first I did everything myself. But as my business has grown, I'm now able to outsource some of the functions. For instance, I have a CPA, Joe Lutz, who does my taxes and payroll. (While I don't have any employees, I have registered recently as an S-Corporation, meaning I'm an employee of my own company and take a salary. I even get a W-2 form. Joe takes care of all of that for me.)

I also hire a firm to handle my listings' showings. That takes a tremendous burden off me and eliminates numerous phone calls from buyer agents every day.

I didn't have an *aha* moment when I knew I was going to be successful. Each year when I did more business than the year before, that was promising.

Not that I'm all about beating my previous numbers every year. That isn't what drives me. What really motivates me is doing good things for my clients. When I do that, the money follows naturally.

It comes down to providing customer services and doing more than people expect of you.

The thing I'm most proud of is that seven times in recent years I've been named one of Denver's top Realtors by *5280* magazine. What's so important about that is that the ratings are based on customer reviews. My clients feel strongly enough about the service I provide them that they're willing to take the time to fill out a survey and tell the magazine how happy they are with me.

That's the greatest testament I could ever receive.

Chapter 4
For First-Time Buyers

One of the joys of what I do is helping people buy their first home.

I truly believe that everyone should live the American dream and own their own home, which is why I named my company American Dream Realty.

Studies have shown that neighborhoods with high rates of owner occupancy are more stable than other neighborhoods, and that properties are better taken care of because the owner occupants have skin in the game. There's also evidence that being a homeowner contributes to more personal satisfaction with life than renting, and that it contributes to higher self-esteem.

In 1995, the Clinton administration established what it called the National Homeownership Strategy. The introduction to the paper reads:

Homeownership is a commitment to strengthening families and good citizenship. Homeownership enables people to have greater control and exercise more responsibility over their living environment.

Homeownership is a commitment to community. Homeownership helps stabilize neighborhoods and strengthen communities. It creates important local and individual incentives for maintaining and improving private property and public spaces.

From a community standpoint, but also from a personal standpoint, buying a home makes all kind of sense for anybody who can afford it. Just consider these benefits:

Many of the benefits are financial, but not all of them. For instance, studies have shown that if you purchase a home close to where you work, you're happier overall. There's also the satisfaction you experience from owning your own residence.

From a financial standpoint, you may be able to purchase a home for less of an upfront investment than renting.

Think about it. To rent a home or apartment, you generally have to put up the first and last month's rent, plus a security deposit amounting to a month's rent. In Denver as of January 2018, the average rental rate is more than $1,500. That means you need $4,500 just to get the keys to your place.

But when you purchase, you may be able to get into your new home with little or no upfront money. The Colorado Housing and Finance Authority (CHAFA) has programs that can help people purchase a home, including 100 percent financing for some people. Other programs provide grants for the down payment. The best way to discover what's out there is to contact a Realtor such as myself.

You can get more information on CHAFA at coloradofirsttimehomebuyer.com.

You can get an FHA loan for 3.5 percent down. And if you're a veteran you can get a VA loan for nothing down.

There are all kinds of other assistance programs available. For instance, you can have the down payment gifted to you as long as you receive a gift letter stating that the donor, typically a parent or other family member, doesn't expect the money back.

The point is that it may be easier than you think to get into your own home and begin realizing the American dream.

A second huge benefit of owning is that when you rent, you're putting the money into somebody else's pocket. You're paying your landlord's mortgage, and in today's inflated rental market, helping make him rich as well. You may as well be throwing the money down a deep, dark hole.

You get none of it back (except the security deposit if you leave the place in good condition. And because of inflation, the sum you get back will be worth less than when you originally put it up, maybe a lot less depending on how long you've stayed.)

But when you own your home, a percentage of your monthly mortgage will come back to you (when you sell) or your heirs. Let's say you purchase a $200,000 home and live there for 30 years. If the traditional inflation rate holds, after 30 years it will be worth over $443,000.

And you'll own it free and clear. You or your children will receive a financial windfall.

And guess what: The profit you realize from the sale of your primary residence can be tax-free (up to certain limits; as of 2017, $250,000 for a single person and $500,000 for a married couple). So the $243,000 profit would be worth another $108,000 or so in practical terms. That's another benefit the government provides to homeowners.

There's more. When you rent, you're paying with tomorrow's inflated dollars. Say you rent an apartment today for $1,500. The landlord will almost certainly raise the rent every year. In 10 years, the payment may be $2,000 or even more if the rental market remains as tight as it is now. And it'll probably keep going up.

Your mortgage principal and interest payment, by contrast, will never go up if you have fixed-rate loan. In fact, during the term of the loan there may be opportunities to refinance and lower your payment.

But if you take out a 30-year fixed-rate mortgage, your principal and interest payment will be the same for your 360th payment as for the first, though over time the balance between interest and principal will change, with more and more of your payment going toward principal.)

At this point, let me explain what goes into your mortgage payment. There are four elements: principal, interest, property taxes and homeowner's insurance (shortened to PITI).

Your mortgage company collects the funds for the insurance and taxes, puts the money into an escrow account and pays them on your behalf.

As I mentioned, in a fixed-rate mortgage, the principal and interest payment will be the same for the life of the loan. But the escrow payment for the insurance and taxes may change.

Typically, if the value of your home increases, so will your property taxes. Insurance rates also could go up at any time. Both would affect your mortgage payment.

Of course, there's always the option to take out an adjustable-rate mortgage, with a lower upfront interest rate, to help you purchase your first home, but you're better off speaking to a mortgage loan officer than me to discuss that issue.

I will say this: There are two obvious circumstances where it may be to your advantage to take out an adjustable loan, some of which don't reset the interest rate for as long as seven years. First, if you don't anticipate being in your home long. And second, if you anticipate a significant increase in your income.

What I'm getting at here is twofold: One, becoming a homeowner benefits you in so many ways, and two, you may be able to purchase a home even if you think you can't.

That's where I come in. I think I love working with first-time buyers more than any other clients. For one thing, I want them to have a great experience, not the type of experience I had the first few times I purchased homes.

I've had so many people say to me they're interested in purchasing a home but don't know where to start. It seems so complex and complicated, they're almost overwhelmed.

The first thing I tell them is that it really isn't as complicated as it seems. And the second thing I tell them is that I can answer all their questions and make the process as comfortable for them as I can.

And that's what I'm going to do right now: Outline the process of becoming a homeowner.

The first thing to think about is whether it makes sense for you to become a homeowner. It usually does, but not always.

If you think you might be moving within a few years, it probably doesn't pay to purchase a home. Most experts say it takes three to four years to recover the closing costs, so if you don't intend to stay put at least that long, you may as well rent.

And if you're moving to a new city, it might make sense to rent for a while until you find out more about the area, explore neighborhoods and get a good idea of where you might want to live.

One final word about the decision on whether to buy: If you have wanderlust, don't like to stay in any one place for too long, I wouldn't become a homeowner. Owning a home does tie you down to some extent and reduces your flexibility.

That's always part of my conversation with first-time buyers. I obviously don't make the decision for them, but I point out the positives and the few negatives of owning a home, and sometimes I advise them that they would be better off in a rental. I have no problem doing this. I'm always about what's right for my clients, not what's best financially for me.

Once you've considered all these factors and decided you want to purchase a home, the first thing is to think about your credit score. Lenders hate risk, and a person's credit score indicates the probable level of risk a lender will be facing in granting you a mortgage.

Your FICO (Fair Isaac Corporation) score determines your ability to get a loan and the interest rate you'll pay. The scores run from 300 to 850, but only if your score is 640 or better will most banks consider lending you money. (There are some exceptions, but loans to those with lower credit scores come with higher interest rates.) To get the best terms, your score should be 740 or higher.

By the way, the actual score you receive from Fair Isaac is often lower than what you get from publicly available sources. This is because, when actual money is on the line, the lenders use stricter criteria, thus potentially lowering the credit score.

Three reporting agencies collect your financial data and issue credit scores: Equifax, Experian and TransUnion. Your score will differ slightly from agency to agency because their criteria are slightly different, but they'll all be roughly comparable.

The factors that go into your credit score include the length of your credit history, your history of paying your bills on time, the amount of money you owe and the types of credit you use.

You can receive your credit score free once a year through annualcreditreport.com.

You can get more detailed information from many different sources.

So you've received your credit score and you've discovered that it needs a little work. Here's where you should approach a mortgage officer. A good officer will show you exactly how you can improve your score. It may take time and it will take discipline and work, but almost anybody can end up with a high enough score to qualify for a loan. Sometimes, small changes can make a big difference.

The next step is to figure out what your buying power is; in other words, how much house you can afford.

I can give you a rough idea based on your income and your other debts, but the best source for this, again, is a mortgage loan officer.

Here's where you'll get into your debt-to-income ratio, which is your gross (pre-tax) income divided by your total debt.

This includes credit card debt, car loans, student debt, consumer loans, etc. Most mortgage lenders will allow no more than a 43 percent debt-to-income ratio. So if your monthly income is $5,000, your total debt load couldn't exceed $2,150.

If necessary, then, a good first step would be to start paying down your debts, especially high-interest credit cards.

Once you've visited with a lender and figured out how much of a loan you can afford, you should get prequalified.

Armed with a prequalification letter, we can compete for listings against other potential buyers. Without that, we don't have much of a chance.

Even better, get preapproved. This involves a lot more documentation and paperwork, but it gives us even more of a competitive advantage against other buyers.

Your lender will tell you exactly what paperwork you'll need to provide, but the major items will be tax returns for the last two years, bank account and investment account statements, W-2 forms, and statements from credit cards and other creditors.

Let me add a note of caution: It's not necessarily a good idea to max out your loan. Don't allow yourself to be house-rich but cash-poor. Just because the bank says you're eligible for a $2,000 mortgage payment doesn't mean you should borrow that much. You want to have enough cash to handle all your other expenses without stress, as well as putting some money away each month.

And don't forget that owning a home comes with maintenance expenses.

If the furnace needs servicing, you pay for it, not the landlord. If your home needs new carpets or fresh paint, it's on you.

And so on.

I can give you rough advice on the issue of how much you can afford, but in the end it's your decision.

Once you're past that hurdle, and you know how much home you can comfortably afford, the next thing to think about is where you want to live and what kind of residence you want. Do you want a single-family home? A condo or townhome? A ranch or a split-level or a tri-level?

Every decision you make now affects your quality of life later. I'll go into depth with you later in the book to help you make these decisions.

In the next chapters, I discuss where we go once you've made those decisions, what I ask of you during the transaction process, and what I will do to ensure the successful completion of your purchase.

Chapter 5
What I Do
For My Clients

I'm a full-service real estate agent, meaning I help my clients through every stage of a real estate sale, whether I'm representing the buyer or the seller.

So the short answer to the question of what I do for my buyers and sellers is this: Whatever it takes to successfully complete the transaction.

That's why I say I provide "service on steroids."

On a more down-to-earth level, there are specific things real estate agents need to do to make sure a transaction goes through.

Let's discuss a fictional sale where I'm the listing agent, and another one in which I'm the buyer's agent. While these transactions aren't real, the situations that arise are typical. Hardly any transaction goes smoothly from start to finish.

I'm the Listing Agent

I was referred to the imaginary Mr. and Mrs. Schaffer by a past client, with whom I had successfully bought and sold multiple properties. This is typical, by the way. Most of my customers are repeat buyers or sellers or referrals from my clients.

The Schaffers had lived for 30 years in their lovely

two-story cottage in Denver's Washington Park area, one of Denver's hottest neighborhoods. They bought it in the 1970s, when the Denver economy was in the dumps. They got a great deal on it, and their home has been wonderful for them. There they raised their three children, who are now all college graduates and successful professionals.

They loved their home, but now that they were retired, both in their 70s, and not interested in maintaining the home. So they decided to move into a senior apartment complex.

They called me on the recommendation of one of Mr. Schaffer's business associates with whom he has remained close since retiring. I had bought and sold homes for this gentleman and his family for more than two decades.

After profusely thanking my past client, I went to the Schaffers' Washington Park home. They told me that I was one of three agents they were considering to list their home. That was fine with me. I have no problem with competition.

As we were getting acquainted in their comfortable living room over cookies and coffee, they told me that they hadn't needed a Realtor since buying their home 30 years ago.

They hadn't had a great experience with their agent, who they thought condescended to them, didn't communicate with them often enough and seemed interested only in the money. That had soured them on the real estate profession.

I told them their story was similar to mine. In my case, having had negative experiences with two agents, I decided to go into the business myself and practice real estate the way I thought it should be done.

They seemed to respond to my personal story, and we built rapport as the evening went on.

I was enjoying myself so much, I almost hated to get down to business.

But after all, that's why I was there, so I began by asking them why they wanted to sell.

People at different stages in their life have different answers to this critical question. Some have outgrown their home and want to move into a bigger one. Some just want to change neighborhoods. Some are relocating because of a new job. Some are getting divorced and need to sell the home and divide the proceeds. Some, like the Schaffers, are downsizing.

Whatever the answer to that question, it determines how I proceed. One aspect of the sellers' motivation is particularly critical: Do they *need* to sell or do they *want* to sell? The corollary is this: How quickly do they need to sell? If they're in no hurry, we may list it at a higher price and be more picky in evaluating offers, but if they need to sell right away, we may employ a strategy called "pricing to sell." This means listing it at less than the maximum dollar and hoping to get it sold quickly.

By the way, I never disclose this information about the sellers to potential buyers or their agents. As a fiduciary for the sellers, I'm legally obligated to work in their best interest, and revealing this critical information to buyers is definitely not in the sellers' interest. But even if there were no legal obligation to protect my sellers' privacy, I would do so because it's the right and ethical way to act.

In the Schaffers' case, they didn't literally need to sell.

Since they could move into their new senior apartment at any time, my thinking was that they should list it on the high side, with the option of reducing the price if the home didn't generate much action in the first few weeks.

After visiting with the Schaffers, I toured the two-level, three-bedroom home. It was in good shape and had been well-maintained, but it was somewhat dated. The kitchens, with Formica countertops, and bathrooms, with old-fashioned avocado green fixtures, were out of style, the carpeting was a little bit worn and the whole home needed a paint job. But it appeared to be sound structurally.

The Schaffers told me that one of the agents had recommended updating the home to the tune of tens of thousands of dollars. The investment would more than pay off, this agent told them.

In some markets, I would have agreed with him. If we had been in a buyer's market, with more homes on the market than home-seekers, it would have been a good strategy.

But the market we were in then was a strong seller's market, meaning there were more buyers seeking fewer homes.

Sometimes homes were under contract within a day of being listed.

My opinion, which I told the Schaffers, was that it wouldn't pay to shell out that kind of money for a home that we could sell easily if it were priced well for its condition.

During the tour, we went into the basement. The Schaffers seemed reluctant to talk too much, and I could tell there was something they were worried about. I pressed them, and they admitted that a few years before, during a summer of constant thunderstorms, the basement had flooded. One other agent had advised them that they didn't need to disclose the problem, but I told them otherwise.

Anything that relates to the condition of the home must be disclosed, I said. To do otherwise is not only against the law, it could expose the sellers and their agent to a lawsuit if the buyers discover the problem (which they always do).

After further discussion, I learned that the Schaffers had put a sump pump in the crawl space and hadn't had any flooding since. I advised them to disclose the flood and show what they had done to avoid a repeat. I was sure that since the problem was fixed, it wouldn't impede the sale.

Only after the tour, the disclosure discussion and my probe of their motivation and their personal circumstances did we discuss price. For some agents, that's the starting point. That's a red flag; it tends to indicate that only the money motivates them.

I didn't ask the Schaffers what the other agents had suggested for the listing price. That would have been unethical.

Instead, I tapped into my knowledge of the Denver real estate market, and in particular the market in Washington Park. Before visiting the couple, I had researched real estate activity in the neighborhood, collecting data on similar homes sold recently, and I had a good idea what the house would sell for.

I felt that it would sell for roughly $900,000. That was the average of similar homes sold in the neighborhood in the previous six months. So in accord with my belief that we should list it a little high, I suggested $910,000.

That brings me to a crucial point: In real estate, listing agents don't set the sale price. That's established by the market. A home will sell for what buyers are willing to pay for it.

That's why you should be wary of agents who advertise that they have some fantastic marketing scheme that results in homes being sold for tens of thousands of dollars more than the asking price. There is no magic wand, or magic marketing program, that an agent can wave that will increase the selling price. Buyers will pay what buyers will pay.

The Schaffers thought the $910,000 figure was low. Maybe so, but I would rather go that way than list it too high and miss out on potential buyers who then won't ever see the home. The couple volunteered that both of the other agents had suggested a higher listing price.

Sometimes in this situation I'll stand firm on the price. If I strongly feel it would not be in the sellers' interest to list at the higher price, I'll tell them so. If they continue to insist on the high price, I'll bow out of the competition and politely suggest that they hire another agent.

In this case, though, since we were in such a hot market, I decided it wouldn't be a bad idea to list it at $935,000. I told them that if we did that, they should be prepared to drop the price to $910,000 if we didn't get any offers in the first month. I didn't want to wait too much longer than that for fear the listing would go "stale," and that buyer's agents would be reluctant to show the home.

The Schaffers agreed with my strategy and agreed to engage my services.

We signed a standard listing contract (drawn up by the Colorado Real Estate Commission). I would be the exclusive listing agent for the property for six months. Some agents ask for a longer contract, but I believe six months is just about right.

I told them right off the bat that if, as time went on, we had different ideas about what was expected of me, I'd be happy to discuss it with them, and if we couldn't come to an agreement, I'd let them out of the contract.

That said, I've never had a seller client end an agreement prematurely. There have been cases where I "fired" clients because they became impossible to work with, they and I had different expectations and they were unreasonable, but I've very rarely had to do that either.

I asked the Schaffers what I always ask my clients, which is how they prefer to communicate. Younger clients typically would rather do it by text or e-mail, but the Schaffers preferred phone calls.

Once I had the listing agreement in hand, I went to work.

I hired a photographer to take high-quality pictures of the home, both interior and exterior. I wanted to wait to place the listing into the Multiple Listing Service (MLS) until I had photos so that the listing would appear in the best light.

Normally I would put a For Sale sign in the yard, but the Schaffers didn't want one and I went along with their wishes.

I advised them on having the home ready to show. I told them to keep it swept and vacuumed, to always make the beds and hide the dirty dishes in the dishwasher.

I told them to be especially aware of the first impression their home made, and to keep the entryway neat, clean and freshly painted. I told them it would be best for them not to be present when their home was being shown. The Schaffers agreed to all of it.

I knew I was going to enjoy working with them, and as the transaction went on, I was proven to be right.

I placed the listing, with photos, on realtor.com, the No. 1 real estate site, and a few other sites including the Denver MLS (multiple listing service) and other sites, including Zillow, Trulia and nextdoor.com. Since this was a high-end property, I also put the listing in a website that specializes in luxury listings. In the old days I would have advertised in the newspaper or in a luxury home magazine, but these days I don't consider print advertising a wise use of my resources.

The next phase of my marketing program involved letting other agents know of my new listing. I have an e-mail list of other agents to whom I send notices of listings. Who knows if one of them might not have just the right buyer? I personally called a handful of agents who work with high-end clients.

I called the company to whom I contract the showing process. That's one of the few elements of my business that I outsource. I placed a lockbox on the front door to which showing agents had the code. Agents were advised to call the company, not me, when they had a potential buyer.

And they were instructed that only qualified buyers would get in the door. We didn't want a bunch of curious looky-loos tromping through the home. The showing service verifies the agents requesting the showing and sets the appointments.

The company informed me when the home had been shown. I have a form for agents to fill out with their buyers' impression of the property. If they don't fill out the form I'll call the agent to get the buyers' input. What I find out from these surveys sometimes helps me market the home differently or suggest other changes that will make it show better.

Since we had the home priced right–that is, just a little bit above what I had originally suggested–we started getting showings immediately. We didn't get as many, of course, as a more moderately priced home would, but for a property at that price range, the action was fairly steady.

Within three weeks, we had two legitimate offers (and one for only $800,000. I knew the Schaffers would reject it out of hand, but I'm bound by law to present all offers to the sellers, no matter how outlandish they may seem). Both of the legitimate couples had viewed the home several times, on different days and at different times. One offer was for $935,000, the other was for $930,000.

I sat down with the Schaffers and together we evaluated the offers. While one was a bit higher, that wasn't the only factor we considered.

I visited with both buyer's agents. There should never be any direct contact at this point between sellers and buyers. Ideally they shouldn't meet until the closing. The sellers were reassured that both couples were extremely well-qualified financially. Both agents liked their buyers a lot, and said they were pleasant people, which was important to the Schaffers because they wanted to sell their home to people who would be good neighbors.

There wasn't a lot to choose between the two couples. But the couple who made the lesser offer won the Schaffers' hearts with a letter explaining why they loved the home so much, how they would enjoy raising their children there and entertaining their friends and families.

That's a strategy that's fairly new, but fairly widely practiced these days, and it can make a difference to the sellers. I call them love letters. The can give the sellers a sense of who'll be living in the home where they've been so happy.

The letter turned the tide for the Schaffers, who accepted the $930,000 offer. While they were leaving $5,000 on the table, I wholeheartedly agreed with them (not that it would have made any difference if I hadn't). The Schaffers were happy to turn over their home to this couple.

We had the buyers sign a standard purchase contract (again, written by the Colorado Real Estate Commission), with a closing date in 30 days. We asked for $10,000 in earnest money. This is more than standard, but not unreasonable given the value of the property. I placed the money in escrow and the buyers would forfeit it if they failed to complete the purchase. When the sale went through, they would receive a $10,000 credit toward the down payment.

The buyers ordered an inspection. I did not attend and never do on my listings. However, I do attend inspections on behalf of my buyer clients.

I asked the buyer's agent to keep me informed when the buyers completed the steps necessary for the sale: nailing down the loan, obtaining homeowner's insurance and title insurance, the transmission of the earnest money to the title company, when an appraisal is ordered.

The buyer's agent was a little bit poky getting back to me at times, but I was persistent and made sure his buyers were following through and keeping the sale on track.

On the day we were set to close, I gathered at the title company with my sellers, the buyers, their agent and the closer (an employee of the title company) to sign the purchase and loan documents. It can be done separately, but it's customary that the buyers and sellers sit down together. Generally this is the first time the buyers and the sellers will have met.

My sellers were a little bit stressed because there was some minor problem with the loan. I assured them that this wasn't uncommon and that the title company would figure it out without too much delay.

And that's the way it went. The delay was less than 30 minutes.

My happy sellers collected the proceeds of their sale. They had already moved into their new apartment and their home was ready for its new owners. I had recommended a cleaning service to make it spotless.

In prior days in Colorado, possession of the home took place three days after the closing, but that has recently changed and now the buyers get the keys at closing. This can be a problem if the sale falls through at the last minute and the sellers have already moved out, but nobody ever said it was a perfect world.

By the way, I didn't help the Schaffers move. That's the one thing I don't do, because if I did it for one client I'd have to do it for all of them.

I'm the Buyers' Agent

The Moores, a couple in their early 30s with two children, found me through my website (www.theamericandreamfinder.com). They had been transferred to Denver a year before and had been renting, but now, with Karen Moore pregnant with their first child, they knew it was time to move into their own home in a good school district and start establishing some roots.

Since they had been homeowners in Santa Fe, N.M., where they had lived before coming to Denver, they were familiar with the process of purchasing a home. So I didn't need to educate them or hold their hands too much. [See Chapter 4 on first-time homebuyers for an explanation of how to get started in purchasing a home.]

When I first talked to Larry Moore, I asked him if he and Karen were prequalified for a mortgage. I highly encourage my buyers to take this step. When they do, they know exactly what their purchasing power is and how much home they can afford. I used to run the numbers with my buyers and informally advise them of how much they could afford, but of late I've decided to leave that up to the mortgage lenders, who know their business much better than I do. Not only that, I have no need to have this personal and private information about my clients.

As it turns out, the Moores, who both had good professional jobs, were prequalified for $400,000. They didn't want to push their credit to the max, though, and said they thought they wanted to look at houses in the neighborhood of $350,000.

I told them that was smart, and that they could get a very nice house in a great area for that price.

They wanted to live in the northern Denver suburbs, which is the main area where I work. Their major concern was having quality schools to send their children to, so I directed them to a website that evaluated school districts and they did the research themselves.

I didn't try to influence them or guide them to any particular district or neighborhood.

At this point, I probed their desires for features and amenities. They were firm on some of their criteria: They wanted three bedrooms and two baths, a single-family home with a good-sized yard where the kids could play and have friends over. They were flexible on the rest of it.

Once they selected the general area where they wanted to buy, I did my own research. I pulled the records of recent sales in the area. I already had a good idea of what the market was doing, but my research confirmed that there were plenty of homes listed that met their criteria.

I entered their e-mail address into the MLS and set it up for them to receive an e-mail when homes matching their criteria hit the market. This enabled them to stay on top of active listings.

They wanted to look at homes right away, so I asked them to sign a buyer agreement. This named me as their sole buyer agent. The contract was for six months, but I told the Moores, like I tell all my clients, that if they ever had serious disagreements over what their expectations were of me, I'd let them out of it.

We set an appointment to view homes the following Saturday. Since we were in a seller's market, I advised them to be ready to make an offer fast if they saw the right home.

In other markets, my advice would have been different.

I identified three homes to look at first. All three were listed at $325,000 to $355,000.

I met them at the first home. They didn't seem to like it, so I questioned them at some depth about what they thought of it. It was a newer home that was cold and didn't have much charm, they thought. And the only tree in the yard was small and didn't cast much shade.

That told me a lot. They were looking for a home with mature landscaping in an established neighborhood. I did mention to them that older homes often came with more mechanical or structural problems than a newer home. They said they were well aware of this and were willing to accept it. The payoff was that they'd be getting a home that had been well-lived in and was pulsing with character.

Neither of the other two homes I had identified for our first showings matched those criteria either, but I said we should go ahead and view them anyway just to give me more of an idea of what they did and didn't like. Their feedback on each of the homes helped me refine the search and identify more suitable properties for the Moores.

A week later, I got a call from Karen Moore. They'd been e-mailed a listing that seemed perfect for them and wanted to see it as soon as possible. I had noticed the same listing and had been ready to call them.

Though it was already late afternoon on a Friday, I told Karen we should go see it immediately. I knew there weren't many homes like it on the market and that it would go fast. Sometimes in the real estate game, the first buyer to make the offer wins the prize.

I knew we'd be dealing with rush-hour traffic, so I asked the Moores to meet me at the home in an hour.

It was a 1900-era cottage with a wraparound porch and a large yard with enormous oak and ash trees, and a flower garden at the front entrance.

The Moores were so excited that they wanted to make an offer on the spot.

Whoa, I said. You haven't even seen the interior, and it's a bad idea to fall so in love with a home right away that you don't see the problems it may have or lose your objectivity.

They were equally charmed when they saw the interior. It had hardwood floors, a large walk-in closet in the master bedroom, newer kitchen appliances and updated bathrooms. In all, I thought it combined modern conveniences with old-time solid construction and attention to detail.

It looked good structurally to me, but I strongly advised the Moores to engage an inspector. These professionals often see things that laymen like me might miss.

After we viewed the entire house, the Moores were more excited than ever. They again insisted on making an offer, and this time I agreed with them. I had a standard real estate purchase contract on my tablet. I went over some of the provisions with the couple and had them sign it electronically.

The only contingencies were the Moores' ability to obtain financing (which I had no doubt they would) and the inspection. The home was listed at $340,000, but I thought it would be fine to offer $10,000 above the asking price and they agreed.

I immediately called the listing agent and told her I had an offer for her. I transmitted it to her electronically and we went through it together over the phone.

She mentioned that she already had two offers, and that they would be accepting offers through the weekend and would evaluate them the following week.

This confirmed what I had already suspected, that this would be a hot listing with a lot of action. Fortunately, my clients had agreed to do something that I now advocate all my buyers do. They would write a "love letter" to the sellers, telling them how much they loved the house, that they planned to bring up their children there and that they felt right about the neighborhood.

I asked the Moores to write the letter by Saturday and e-mail it to me so that I could forward it to the listing agent. I didn't write the letter for them, but I gave them some advice. Selling your home is just about the most emotional business transaction anybody is involved in, I said, so write the letter to appeal to their emotions.

I immediately forwarded the letter to the listing agent.

We waited impatiently through the weekend. I called the listing agent again on Sunday and learned that there had been five more offers. She would be discussing them with her clients in the morning and said we should have an answer by Monday afternoon.

Waiting to hear whether an offer has been accepted is one of more nerve-wracking aspects of real estate– more so for my clients than for me. It doesn't affect me as much as it does them, but I still feel anxiety for them because I care so much about my clients.

I've had numerous offers turned down in my career. But not this one.

The listing agent called at 5 p.m. with the good news. Financially my clients' offer was competitive with others, but it was the letter that made the difference. Like most sellers, they wanted to have their home in the hands of people who'd be good neighbors and would take care of the property.

That was the Moores.

I had my clients write a check for the earnest money and delivered it to the title company. The closing was set for 60 days hence.

Now the Moores had to get to work. While they had been prequalified for a loan, now they had to receive final approval. Again, I didn't anticipate any problems with that.

They had to obtain homeowners' insurance. I recommended an agent I knew, a broker who has access to several insurance companies, but they already had a relationship with an insurance agent, so that was fine. They also had to have all the utilities at their new home placed in their name as of the closing date.

A week after the offer was accepted, I checked in with the Moores to make sure they were taking care of everything they needed to.

To my surprise, it was all done. Their credit was already approved. My clients aren't always so much on the ball, and sometimes need several prompts. I'll stay on top of them as much as I need to, but in the Moores' case, it wasn't necessary.

The next step was the inspection. I've heard of buyers sometimes waiving inspections in hot markets, but I think that's foolish and never advise my clients to forego the inspection. This is especially critical in an older house.

On the day the inspection was scheduled, I met the inspector and my buyers.

Some buyer agents don't take this step, but it's just part of my standard service.

The inspection confirmed what I had observed, that the home had been well-taken care of and that it was structurally sound. He discovered only a few minor problems, nothing serious enough that we needed to ask the sellers to fix them.

That's not always the case, of course. Sometimes the inspection exposes serious problems. If the sellers aren't willing to fix them, I sometimes advise my clients to back out of the transaction. Assuming there has been an inspection contingency clause in the purchase contract, which is standard, the buyers can back out without losing their earnest money.

With the buyers' credit approved, the next step was the appraisal. If it didn't come in high enough, the bank would only lend up to the appraised price. The buyers might then have to either come up with enough cash in the down payment to cover the difference or give up on the purchase. Conversely, the sellers could agree to lower the price to the appraised value.

But in my analysis of the property that I performed after the Moores expressed interest in it, but before they made an offer, I had figured the appraisal would be favorable.

And it was.

After the inspection and appraisal, the Moores' loan was formally approved.

Now we had everything ready to close the sale. On closing day I showed up at the title company along with my buyers, the sellers and their agent and the closer. Three days earlier, my buyers had received the disclosure forms itemizing all their costs and the monthly mortgage payment. They had taken the necessary steps to wire the down payment and closing costs to the title company.

They signed document after document (only a few of which really mattered; the rest were more or less pro forma documents). The most important form was the loan agreement, in which they pledged to remit the mortgage payment every month.

This form is known as the "if you don't pay, you don't stay" document.

All the proceeds of the sale having been disbursed, I said "see you later" to the Moores, agreed with the listing agent that it would be fun to work with her again, and we all went off to our separate lives.

Chapter 6
What I Need From My Clients

In previous chapters, I've discussed all that I do for my buyers and sellers. This chapter covers what I need from them in return.

Buying or selling a house is very much a collaborative process. I'm ready to give it everything I have, even going beyond what most agents are willing to do, but without the right kind of cooperation from my clients, we don't end up getting anything accomplished. The whole thing becomes a waste of my time, and theirs.

And I'm not a big fan of wasting time. We all have the same 24 hours a day, and spending big chunks of these hours unproductively is not what I want to be doing.

So here's what I ask of my clients.

First, have an open mind. I don't want them thinking they have to do exactly as I suggest, but I do expect them to acknowledge my expertise and my experience and not come to me thinking they already know everything about real estate.

I'll put it this way: I want my clients to be in control of their own sale or purchase, but be willing to be guided and to respect my judgment.

Second, have trust in me. Obviously trust has to be earned, and I spend every second I'm on the job earning my clients' trust. Once I've earned it, my clients should believe that I'm in it for them. I'll never do or suggest anything that would be in my interest but not in the interest of my clients.

Another really good thing to have is thick skin—especially for sellers. Selling your home is probably the most emotional transaction anybody goes through. (Buying can be emotional too, but not in the same guttural way that selling is.)

And it *should* be an emotional experience. After all, this may be the place where you and your spouse have transitioned from newlyweds to forever companions, where your love deepened and broadened, where you raised your children, where you shared treasured times with friends and family, maybe even where some of your loved ones died.

You've lovingly maintained it, chosen just the right furnishings and decorations, and you have a deep attachment to it. Every mark on the wall, every gouge in the hardwood floor, your home's every quirk, bring back fond memories.

So when it comes time to sell and buyers don't seem willing to pay what it's worth in your mind, or unwilling to negotiate, or when you don't get very many offers at all, you're going to get angry or depressed, or both.

That's only natural. But it's my job to be the unemotional mediator, working in your best interests despite the state of your emotions. People in a highly emotional state can make bad decisions, and I must steer them away from a decision that will be harmful.

I also make sure my clients know right at the start that there's every chance the transaction will develop road bumps. I've hardly ever overseen a transaction that went completely smoothly, with no problems whatsoever. But almost any problem can be overcome, and that's what I make sure my clients understand. Then when issues arise, we can take them in stride, solve them and move forward.

Another thing I desire, if not demand, from my clients is loyalty. (I usually receive it.) I work my butt off for them and do everything in my power to become their Realtor for life. In return, I hope that my clients refer me to their friends and family, and that the next time they need real estate services, they call me.

I sold a home to a couple in Westminster in 1997. They've kept my name and phone number ever since, and in 2006 – 19 years later! – I sold their home and helped them buy another home. They're my kind of clients.

With these big concepts out of the way, let's get down to the nitty gritty. In any real estate transaction, there are certain things buyers and sellers must do. These have nothing to do with loyalty, open-mindedness or trust, but they simply must occur for the transaction to go through.

Let's take buyers first.

In my initial meetings, I ask them to contact a lender so they can get prequalified for a loan.

Based on the information I get from the lender, I'll have a pretty good idea of how much money they'll be able to borrow. In a perfect world, they will already have submitted their financial documents to the lender and gotten a good idea how much they can afford to pay. If they qualify for a $300,000 house but they want to look at $800,000 homes, I'll try to bring them down to earth. If they won't listen to me, I'll let them go and let some other agent deal with their unrealistic expectations.

The next step is to discuss what type of home they're looking for. This is partly dependent on their finances and how much they can afford to pay. We'll talk that all out at the very beginning. In most cases, I like my buyers to be prequalified by a lender for a specific amount. That tells me exactly what type of homes, in which locations, to be looking for.

Once that step is completed, I want my clients to begin thinking about where they want to live and in what kind of home. This is a lifestyle decision as much as a financial one. I can probe their lifestyle to see if we can figure out what type of property works best for them, but in the end it's the buyers who have the final say.

For instance, do they like to entertain or do they spend most of their time with just their family? This tells me a lot. People who like to host parties probably want a home with the amenities they need to have people over: big public spaces, an attractive entrance, a large kitchen, nice landscaping and a large patio and/or balcony for outdoor events. If it's to be mostly the family, these things aren't as important, but a large master bedroom suite with a walk-in closet might be desirable.

If they're not going to be home much, or don't want the burden of yardwork, a townhome or condo might be just right.

Where do they want to live? If they have school-age children, a quality school district is clearly important. If not, that's less of a factor (though the school district is always an important factor in re-selling the house). Do they want a home on a large lot with a nice yard, or a smaller lot with less maintenance? Is there a specific municipality they want to live in? What about distance from work? Is a short commute important or not?

With my help, my buyers will arrive at answers to all these questions. I often serve as a consultant, refining their wants and needs.

Then we'll go out looking at properties. Most of my buyers have certain criteria that we must meet for them to consider a home, along with other criteria that would be nice but aren't essential. They may take a checklist along with them, or a clipboard with a note pad so they can jot down what they like and don't like about each house we visit. Feedback to me after the showings is a big help in selecting which homes to visit in the future, and which ones to let go.

(By the way, part of my "service on steroids" philosophy is that if necessary, I'll go to the home before the buyers get there and let the dog out. Many Realtors won't do this, but in my mind we make pretty darn good money for what we do and I want to do everything I can to earn it. I have this motto on the vision board in my office: "Anything less than 100 percent is a waste of time.")

Once they've selected the home they want, it's time to make an offer. In a super-competitive market such as we've seen in Denver in the 2010s, buyers need to be prepared to move quickly. My buyers have lost many homes because they waited a day or two to make the offer. By then, the home was already taken.

This often becomes a time for thick skin. In a hot market, buyers must be prepared to have offers rejected. Some buyers get rejected multiple times. They can't afford to let this hurt their feelings or get them down. I often become a psychologist at times like this. If they're discouraged, I just tell them to stick with it and eventually they'll get an offer accepted.

I had some buyers recently who wrote 15 great offers, all of which were rejected. That can happen in a market such as we're in right now. But I kept telling them not to get discouraged, and as it turned out I was speaking to another agent who had a listing that hadn't yet gone on the market. I asked if my clients could see before she put it on the market. She agreed, and my clients liked the house and made an offer right away that the sellers accepted.

So now they have an accepted offer. They've found the house they loved, and they've arrived at a mutually agreeable price with the seller. Now they need to get serious about obtaining the loan. (Being prequalified doesn't mean they're accepted.)

Lenders require mountains of paperwork, including tax returns, W-2 forms, bank account and investment fund statements, employment information, and much more. Buyers must get these documents to the lender in timely fashion.

Now we're almost to the closing table. They've had the home inspected and their loan approved, but there are still things they need to do. Obtain homeowner's insurance and title insurance, for instance. I can't do that, and without it they won't be getting the loan.

And for heaven's sake, they can't afford do something silly like buying a car or co-signing on another loan before closing on the home. Many buyers don't know that lenders do a pre-closing check, and if they've added a significant debt since they were approved, they'll quickly be unapproved for exceeding the debt-to-income ratio. And don't try to hide the fact they've have lost their job. The lender will know. (Oh, that pesky closing-day verification!)

On to sellers.

Here's what they need to do:

First, trust me and listen to me when I tell them how much I believe their house is worth. I don't just pick a number out of thin air. I carefully evaluate the home and the neighborhood, the condition of the house, the amenities and what comparable homes have sold for, and I give you my best estimate of what the home will sell for. Ultimately, I don't set the selling price; the market does that. But I have a very good idea what any particular home will bring.

You may think your home is worth considerably more than I do. That's your right, and you'll certainly be able to find an agent who'll list it at whatever price you want. But be very careful in doing that: Some agents' business models call for what we refer to as "buying listings"–in other words, listing homes at a higher price than they know they're worth, and assuring the sellers they can get the desired price while knowing all along that it will need to be reduced. They get the listing over more honest agents who'll give their legitimate and informed opinion of what the listing price should be.

This is unethical, and not something I would ever do. And it works to sellers' disadvantage because their home won't sell at the listed price, and after a home has been on the market for a while, the listing can become "stale."

It's a similar principle to a job-seeker being out of work for many months. After a certain amount of time, employers start to wonder what's wrong with him that he's been out of work for so long. When a home's been on the market for a long time, the same thing's at work: buyers' agents wonder why and can become reluctant to show it.

The upshot is that the price will inevitably be reduced, and the final sales price may be lower than what it could have been had it been listed for the right price in the first place. The agent gets the commission, but he or she hasn't worked in the best interest of the seller.

This isn't to say that I don't sometimes list a house for more than I think it'll sell for, and sometimes it works out for the sellers. Bravo to them.

But when I do that, I make sure the seller knows my opinion of what it's worth. I often obtain an agreement to reduce the price if it hasn't sold in a certain period of time.

Everything's upfront and there's no hidden agenda on my part.

Once we've listed the house, it's time for showings. Sellers need to be flexible in the times they allow the home to be shown. Yes, the showing process is a pain in the butt, especially since it almost always works out better for the sellers to be away during showings. (Not the least of reasons for this is that if they get to talking to the buyers, they may inadvertently give away something that will put me and them at a disadvantage during negotiations.)

Sellers can't make the window for showings so narrow that few people are able to come into the home.

And they need to keep the home in reasonable condition. Make the beds, put the dishes in the cabinets or the dishwasher, keep it as free from clutter as possible.

Some agents advocate removing all personal items from the home; that is, family photos, that weird collection of pigs, or whatever.

The idea is that buyers should be able to see themselves as the home's owner. I understand the thinking that goes into that, but I think having family keepsakes on display does no harm. In fact, I think it makes the home more "homey" and warm, and thus more inviting for buyers.

Some agents and home stagers recommend baking bread or cookies in advance of showings, giving the home a nice aroma.

Again, this doesn't do any harm but I don't know that it really does any good either, and it puts quite a burden on busy sellers. I'd rather just see a clean, well-maintained home.

One thing I do highly recommend is to spiff up the entryway. Keep the front siding and the front door painted, the sidewalks and porch swept and the lawn neatly trimmed. First impressions often matter the most, and overcoming a bad first impression is very difficult. It does no harm to have growing flowers, even if they're only in a pot on the porch.

Another critical aspect of selling your home is disclosure. Anything you know about your home, you must disclose to potential buyers. If there's a crack in the foundation, even if it's not visible, disclose. If the basement floods every spring, disclose. If you've had your electrical system inspected and the electrician says the whole house needs to be rewired, disclose!

Under the law, if a seller knows of a situation that's material to the condition of a home, and doesn't disclose it, and if the buyers find out, they can then sue not only the seller but the seller's agent

And the buyers always find out.

I don't want to be sued! So my rule for my sellers is to tell me everything about the house, whether or not they think it's relevant. I know the disclosure laws and I can decide whether not a condition needs to be revealed.

Although it's not legally required, at least in Colorado, I would ask sellers to disclose if somebody has died in the home. It doesn't automatically make the home uninhabitable, but some people are made uncomfortable, and would steer away from buying a home where that's happened. If they find out after they've made the purchase, it might make them angry.

And I don't want angry buyers.

Chapter 7
Real Estate
Business Models

In this chapter, I discuss some things that you may think are of interest only to Realtors and others in the real estate industry.

I'm talking about business models, commission structures and related topics.

Before you nod off or tune out, let me explain why I'm doing this. It's because these factors are directly related to the services you receive from real estate agents, and how much you pay for them.

Are you interested now?

Let's break it down by broad topic. The first thing I'm going to talk about is the broadest: the ownership of real estate brokerages. There are basically two types of ownership structures: locally owned independents and large franchise operations, which may be regional, national or even international.

My brokerage, American Dream Realty LLC, is in the former category. I run my business as I see fit, only for the benefit of myself and my clients. I don't answer to anybody but myself, and most importantly, the money I earn stays in the community.

By contrast, consider franchise corporations such as Century 21, Coldwell Banker, Keller Williams, RE/MAX and others. They all advertise that their offices are locally owned and operated, which is true. Local broker/owners pay a fee to the corporation for the privilege of using the brand name, and in turn are licensed to take advantage of the corporation's marketing, trademarks, logos and so forth. They receive other services from the corporations, such as training, affiliate relationships, broker support and more.

While local brokers own the offices, they must adhere to the policies and procedures laid down by the franchisor, which vary from company to company.

Agents of the franchise companies pay monthly fees to the broker, who in turn pays the franchise. Thus, a large percentage–varying from corporation to corporation–of the money the agents earn in real estate transactions doesn't stay in the community, but goes to corporate headquarters to enrich the corporation's owners and shareholders.

Almost all of the major real estate franchises are listed on the stock exchange and are thus beholden to Wall Street. One of the last holdouts was RE/MAX, which went public in 2013 after 50 years as a privately owned corporation. One of its advertising mottos was "Main Street, not Wall Street."

Of course, RE/MAX can't say that any more.

Many studies have shown the value of using local independent companies as opposed to chains for your goods and services. One, by the London-based New Economic Foundation, found that twice the money stays home when you buy locally instead of from a chain. While that study related to local food providers vs. chain grocery stores, the same concept could apply to any industry, including real estate.

To sum it up: You can pay me, or another local broker, and benefit the community or you can pay a franchised agent and heavily benefit Wall Street, millionaire or billionaire corporate owners and shareholders.

I'm going to briefly discuss commission structures, which truly are of interest mostly to real estate professionals, but they can have an effect on the service you receive.

The traditional model called for agents to work on a commission split, meaning they returned a percentage of each transaction to the broker–sometimes as much as 50 percent. The broker in turn provided services such as advertising and training that the agents didn't have to pay for.

Then companies including RE/MAX introduced a new concept.

The agents would pay a set fee each month to the broker and then would keep 100 percent of their commissions (or as high a percentage as allowed by state or provincial laws). That concept appealed to high-producing agents, who pay less to the broker that way than with the traditional model.

Most of the industry has now adopted variations of the 100 percent concept. Some have different structures for different agents, such as a commission split early in their careers with the promise that they could advance to the 100 percent concept when they got more experience.

I've worked under both structures, first at Century 21 under a split and later at Metro Brokers under the 100 percent concept.

I preferred the second approach, as do most productive agents, for obvious reasons. You have to wonder how motivated an agent will be to complete a transaction when he knows that a high percentage of his earnings go to somebody else.

Of course, now I pay nothing to my broker, because I'm my own broker.

There's one other structure, rarely seen. Agents are paid a salary rather than a commission. My only comment is this: If agents on a commission split are less motivated to complete the transaction, imagine the motivation of those on a salary, who get paid whether they close the transaction or not. Enough said.

Now I'm going to discuss not corporate business models, but service models. There are just about as many of these as there are real estate brokerages, and more are appearing all the time, but these are the major ones.

Full Service – This means working with both buyers and sellers, and overseeing all aspects of the transaction from contract to closing. Most agents, including myself, offer full real estate services. I think this is the best possible structure both for agents and for consumers. We offer to our clients our experience, our knowledge, our negotiating acumen and our insight into human nature.

What we charge for our services is a percentage of the sale price. For instance, on a $200,000 sale, if the commission is 5.5 percent, the seller would pay $11,000. The listing agent traditionally sets the commission and then offers the buyer's agent half of it. Under the scenario outlined above, each agent would receive $5,500.

There is no set percentage for commissions. In fact, it is illegal under anti-trust laws for agents to even discuss commission percentages with each other.

Buyer or Seller Only – Some agents choose only to work with one or the other segment of the real estate market. That's fine for them, but to me it's a self-defeating strategy. Not only do you decline to work with half the market, thus potentially limiting your income, but you deny yourself the opportunity to be people's real estate agent for life, which is my goal. If you only work with buyers, you won't be able to represent your clients when they need to sell their home, and vice versa.

Limited Service – There are various limited-service models. Some of them include *a la carte* menus (paying only for specific services).

Examples would include paying only for having your listing placed in the Multiple Listing Service (MLS), only to have a contract drawn up, or only to manage showings.

Buyers and sellers can save money in fees this way, but do they really want to? Do they really have the skill and knowledge to perform all the other functions necessary to complete a transaction? Do they have the knowledge of the market, the negotiating skills, the knowledge of real estate law, that Realtors have? Can a buyer or seller representing himself really make a better deal than a trained agent?

Do sellers really want to manage the showing process themselves, not knowing who will be coming into their home?

Discounted Commissions – These may come with or without full service. Think about it: Why would a good agent voluntarily agree to a commission that's less than market rate? The answer is, a good agent wouldn't.

Miscellaneous Models – These include real estate consulting, in which agents charge a flat rate or an hourly rate for giving advice, and transaction coordinators, where agents work only in the interest of the deal, not for either the buyers or the sellers.

In the wake of the hot real estate market we've experienced since 2010, venture capitalists, entrepreneurs and profit-seekers have been flooding into the real estate industry. (Where were they in 2006 through 2009, when the market was in the tank? Nowhere to be seen. But when they think there's major money to be made, here they come.)

There are those who claim technology will transform the real estate industry even more than it already has, and others who claim robots and automation will largely take the place of human real estate agents. There are those who are actively trying to "disrupt" the industry for their own profit.

Let me concede that technology has had a huge effect on our industry, just as it has in every area of our lives. In the old days, before the Internet, MLS listings were published in closely held books that only Realtors had access to. Buyers had to go to Realtors to buy a house, having no other way to identify properties for sale. The only exception was if they made a private deal with a homeowner.

Realtors would drive clients around to look at houses, leading some critics to claim that buyer agents were little more than tour guides. Of course, that was never true. But driving around was a much bigger part of our lives than it is now, when buyers have access to the same information we do. I often hear from clients who want to view a home they saw online.

We have Internet-based real estate brokerages now, with no brick-and-mortar offices.

While it's obvious that technology has had its effect on real estate, almost all of it positive, I can't see robots replacing real people in the process. How can a robot stare down an adversary in negotiations and promise to withdraw from a deal if certain conditions aren't met? How can a robot understand the anguish of a new widow who has to sell the home she's lived in for 50 years? How can a robot get on the phone with a recalcitrant lender and tell him to get his ass in gear?

I can, and have, done all that and my clients have benefited.

Chapter 8

Stories, I Have Stories

When you've been in a business as long as I have, invariably things happen that are funny, sad, poignant and any other emotion you can think of. And in fact, transactions that have stories attached to them are the ones I tend to remember; not the ones that proceed smoothly from beginning to end.

Some of my interesting transactions have involved the closing. That's when the buyers and sellers and their agents gather at the title company to sign documents, transfer funds and turn over the deed to the new owners.

Most of my closings have gone on smoothly and with no issues. After all, both sides want the same thing: for the transaction to go through.

Usually it works this way: The buyers and sellers and their agents sit down at a conference table in a title company closing room with the "closer," the title company employee who facilitates the transaction and distributes the funds to the sellers and the real estate agents. There are other scenarios, such as the buyers and sellers going separately to the title company, but on most occasions the transaction closes with no difficulties.

Oh, you'll occasionally see a wise-ass buyer who thinks he's a comedian. I wasn't the agent at this particular closing some years ago, but what happened is that the agent for the sellers was also representing the same couple as buyers later that day. The agent, then, had two commissions, each worth thousands of dollars, at stake.

The couple needed the proceeds from the sale to purchase their new home.

As described to me by the buyer, everybody was at the table and the closer was explaining the procedure. When she arrived at the point where she said the buyers had to present a check for the down payment and closing costs, the husband got a confused look on his face and said this:

"Was I supposed to bring a check?"

The look on the sellers' agent could best be described as horror. (I would have reacted the same way!) For a fleeting instant, he saw two commission checks flying away and vanishing into the ether.

The buyer, who all along had had a cashier's check in his pocket, quickly admitted that he'd only been playing a little prank. "Just kidding, just kidding!"

The agent didn't exactly appreciate it, but the closing went forward with no more jokes or other issues.

Just occasionally, even more interesting things happen. The cops had to be called to one of my closings. That was one of those interesting moments!

I was the listing agent for a divorcing couple who were selling their house. On closing day, as it happened, the husband was in jail. He didn't want to sell but his soon-to-be ex-wife did.

She went to a judge and asked to be allowed to complete the sale. He agreed, and I got power of attorney to sign on behalf of the husband.

So there we were at the closing table: Mrs. Seller, myself as the listing agent, two attorneys for the seller, the buyers, the buyer's agent, the closer from the title company and the buyer's attorney. The tension in the air was thick. There didn't seem to be enough oxygen in the room.

At one point, attorneys for the two sides got into a verbal dispute. It got so bad that eventually both attorneys called the police.

The closer's eyes sort of glazed over. She had probably seen similar things happen before.

After the police arrived, the situation settled down and it was agreed by everybody that the attorneys were doing more harm than good and that their presence wasn't required. They reluctantly departed the premises and the closing went ahead.

Another day at another closing, I was the agent for a divorced biker couple who were selling a house. He was a big mean old guy and may have been a drug dealer. He just gave me that vibe.

The property they were selling had a resident cat. The ex-Mrs. Biker declared that they couldn't find the stray feline. Mr. Biker heatedly said, "Who cares about the cat?"

Mrs. Biker didn't like that at all. At the start, I had strategically positioned myself between the two, which was a good thing because if I hadn't done that, they might have come to blows.

Another time, I got caught in the middle of a dispute that didn't have anything to do with me. I was the listing agent for some rural acreage near my home of Brighton, Colo. The buyer was a good ol' boy, a Texas oilman.

The adjacent property was owned by a woman who now I won't speak to or even answer her calls. Here's why.

This woman had some cows that were constantly getting onto the seller's property and also onto the road. They had a battle over the whole thing, and the seller discovered that under Colorado law, if animals were habitually getting in the road, they could be rounded up and sold.

So he threatened to take her cows north to Wyoming and auction them off. Essentially he forced her to build a fence (even though he would be the one responsible for putting up a fence to keep animals off his own property). So she put up the fence.

The buyers kept horses on their newly bought property. This woman called me and said that the horses were using her fence! (Exactly how they were "using" it wasn't exactly clear.)

I asked if they were harming the fence or knocking it down and she said no, so I told her there was no problem.

The first time she called me, she ripped me a new one, even though I told her over and over again that it had nothing to do with me. At first I was nice to her, but when she called again I was more familiar with the circumstances and I saw no reason to treat her nicely. I told her if she didn't like what was going on, she could take down the fence. Well, she didn't like that!

We went around and around again for 15 minutes or more. The same flipping conversation!

I finally got rid of her, and now her number is literally programmed into my phone as The Crazy Lady and I won't answer it.

I told the buyer's agent that if she ever got taken to court over the fence issue, I'd stand up for her.

In what can sometimes be an uneasy process, I always appreciate people with a sense of humor. One time an inspector was at the home my client was buying. Whenever I can, I try to be there for inspections.

This home had a big elk head on the wall. The inspector looked at it and said, "Wow, that elk must have been traveling pretty fast when it hit the wall!"

Another time, an honest inspector made me feel good about the business I'm in. My buyer was purchasing a single-family home in Broomfield. We were doing the inspection and the inspector noticed a big crack in the foundation. My buyer, a senior lady whose husband was in a nursing home, said to him, "If I were your mother, what would you tell me to do?"

The inspector hemmed and hawed a little bit, but at last I went outside so he could answer her honestly. He told her, "If I were you I wouldn't buy it." It was the right thing to do, but he must have wondered if he'd ever again get any business from me.

I told him I would never expect him to advise somebody to do something he knew to be wrong. The incident, in fact, caused me to be more likely to recommend him.

My buyer was being forced to leave her own townhome because it was essentially falling down. The builder was buying her out, so she was very sensitive to structural issues. She ended up buying another unit in the same complex that was in good shape.

Many of the interesting things that have happened have occurred during showings. You never know exactly what you're going to get when you walk into a home.

On one showing, there was a skeleton sitting on the couch, seemingly relaxing and enjoying a little leisure. Scared the bejeesus out of my buyer!

Early in my career, a client and I went to look at a house. It was then called a pre-foreclosure (later, when the housing market and the economy collapsed in the late 1990s, it would be referred to as a short sale). This home was full of trash.

In fact, the owners had been hoarders and there was barely a path through all the crap. It was even creepier when we got into the bedroom and saw the black-painted walls.

There was a dog in the backyard. My client had a little girl and the dog bit her. She wasn't seriously injured, but the bite drew blood. Since then, I've been careful to ask if there are any animals on a property I'm showing, and I may refuse to take clients in if there is.

This didn't happen to me, but when I was at Metro Brokers, another agent who was showing a house went out onto the balcony off the master bedroom and locked herself out. She had to jump off the balcony, thankfully only a short hop.

I was showing an investor a home that she wanted to buy for her son.

It was a foreclosure and nobody was living there. There were cockroaches all over the place, and cockroaches are one thing I can't stand.

Neither I nor my client said anything to each other, and we completed the showing. She was new to me and I didn't want to be a wimp. But after we were out, we discovered we had both wanted badly to get out. I said, "I thought you wanted to stay," and she said to me, "I thought you wanted to stay." If only we had communicated better. Afterward we had a good laugh about it because we were both so relieved to be out of that house.

Another showing was a home where the residents were S-and-M enthusiasts (sadism and masochism for the uninitiated). And they didn't bother to hide their toys; there were hooks in the ceiling (which I didn't get until it was explained to me) and explicit pictures on the walls. It didn't particularly bother me or the buyer, but he didn't buy the home.

When I'm the listing agent, I always advise the sellers to be away when their home's being shown. It just works out better that way. A couple of experiences I've had as a buyer's agent have reinforced the wisdom of that strategy.

With my buyer client, I rang the doorbell at this one home, and getting no answer, opened the lockbox, put the key in the door and went in. We checked the kitchen and living room without seeing anybody. But in the bedroom, there was a woman asleep in the bedroom with her baby sitting next to her. We got close enough to see they were both all right and left.

I was showing lofts in downtown Denver, and one time I let my buyer go in first, which I hardly ever do. The buyer went in and saw the resident inside. He gasped, "We have company!" The resident either didn't know or had forgotten that we were coming.

More than once I've gone into a home with a buyer and heard the shower running. One time we just took a quick look around and left. Whoever was in the shower never came out.

Chapter 9
Networking and Connecting

In my more than 20 years as a real estate agent, I've employed various marketing strategies.

As a newbie with Century 21, I was required to make cold calls. That was a somewhat effective strategy then, but times have changed. So many people are on no-call lists now, and many more have only cell phones whose numbers aren't listed. Even people for whom neither of those apply often don't answer their phones unless they recognize the number or the caller.

The upshot is that cold calling basically doesn't work these days, which is fine with me because I never liked to do it anyway. And I certainly don't like being on the other end of cold calls.

I've tried online marketing with limited results. For some time I paid extra money to Realtor.com (the official site of the National Association of Realtors) to enhance the online presentation of my listings with more photos, deeper descriptions and so on.

All to no effect whatever.

There are many websites now that try to connect real estate buyers and sellers to properties and agents. These include probably the best-known, Zillow, and other sites such as Trulia, Redfin, Homes.com, RealtyTrack, HouseValues and many more. They're all different, with different business models and different services, but the common denominator is that they offer free estimated values of homes (which are often wildly inaccurate, and not really worth paying much attention to other than as a very rough indicator) and offer an online way to contact a Realtor, lender or perhaps other real estate professionals.

On most of these sites, Realtors such as myself can pay for better placement. Our names get listed higher on the site, or our listings appear before others who don't pay extra, or whatever specific benefit the site offers. I tried this strategy on Zillow for about a year and a half, and while I may have gotten some business from it, I spent about as much as I made.

The bottom line: This type of online advertising seems to be barely worth the time, effort and money you put into it, at least for me.

I have a Facebook page and a LinkedIn profile that I probably should do more with. I've been trying to gather more information about effectively using social media.

One of my fun marketing gimmicks is personal promotion products. You know what I'm talking about: items with your name, logo and contact information that in theory people will keep around. Common personal promotion items are pens, note pads, refrigerator magnets, calendars and similar items.

I've used keychains with little flashlights, cloths to clean your phone screens, lotion, sunscreen, magnetized dishwasher discs ("Clean" on one side and "Dirty" on the other), boxes of candy and other items. They're not huge money-makers, but in theory they keep my name out there.

I'm currently sending monthly postcards to people in my "farm area" (that is, the neighborhoods close to my Brighton home where I particularly want to do business). I want to start doing some door-knocking in these neighborhoods (called "pop-bys" by some), not so much to generate business as just to get to know people and have them get to know me. A Realtor can never have too much information about what's going on in the areas she serves, and there's no better way to get information than to develop relationships with people living there.

But the best marketing strategy I've discovered, by far, is networking. Real estate, like many industries, is a people business.

In any given neighborhood in the Denver area, there are thousands of Realtors who can help you buy or sell a home.

Most of them will do a good job for you. So how does someone like myself differentiate herself from all those other fine agents?

The first answer is to provide excellent service. I'm not a "churn-and-burner" who never expects to hear from my client again after the transaction is complete, and thus doesn't care about providing good service. So I provide the best service possible to every single one of my clients. I don't think there's any agent anywhere who goes to greater lengths than I to ensure a successful transaction.

Once, for example, I took an older client shopping for a new kitchen table. She didn't want to go alone. Another time, I was at an open house waiting for people to stop by, and decided to wash the windows. I don't do that for everybody, but it was something I felt like doing at the time.

That's why my motto is "service on steroids."

By taking care of my clients to the nth degree, I inspire them to use my services the next time they need to buy or sell, and just as importantly, to refer me to their family and friends.

Thus I have no qualms about marketing myself and my business to other small-business owners, who will in turn (I hope) use my services themselves and recommend me to their acquaintances.

That's where referral groups come in.

They've traditionally been called leads groups, but I think they're more properly named referral groups. A lead is just that: a name of somebody who may or may not be ready to use somebody's services. A referral is a high-quality lead, one where the person is ready to do business and willing to accept a call from a service provider.

The concept of referral groups is simple: Only one representative of each industry is allowed in the group, giving that person a monopoly. Just one Realtor, one insurance agent, one financial advisor, one plumber, one electrician and so on.

Members commit to using their colleagues in the group for their personal needs and to refer them to their acquaintances.

I've been a member of a referral group since 2003, shortly after opening my own shop. My self-esteem was still fairly low coming out of an abusive marriage, but I was enjoying being in real estate and I was interested in expanding my business.

In the early 2000s, I was managing a bar in Brighton part-time, along with pursuing real estate, and the owner hired a bookkeeper named Eric Gardner to help me out with QuickBooks. Gardner was a member of what was then called Colorado Business Leads, an early-day referral group.

I had never attended any sort of networking event, and didn't even know anything about the concept of networking. But Eric invited me to his CBL meeting. I've since learned that this was a great stroke of luck, as there are many Realtors seeking to belong to a referral group, and it's rare for an opening for a Realtor to occur.

He told me the meeting was at 7:30 on Thursday morning. I'm not a morning person and I thought he was smoking crack! But I agreed to go anyway.

Here's how the CBL meeting worked. Each week one or two people would give a 10-minute presentation, giving details of their business and helping their fellow group members give them referrals. Each member would then give a 30-second to one-minute commercial each week.

For me, it was torture. I was shy to the point of near-paralysis. (I know that people who didn't know me then don't believe this. You can't shut me up now.)

Talking in front of all these people I didn't know? I was so freaked out, I couldn't even bring myself to stand up to deliver my commercial.

Well, after the first meeting I discovered I enjoyed the group's rapport. I decided to come back and do it again. I let the bar owner know I'd be coming in later on Thursdays.

And from that point to this day, at 7:30 Thursday morning I'm in my meeting (the group is now called Your Networking Universe).

It took maybe six months before I got comfortable in a networking setting. I discovered that the other members were just like me–small businesspeople doing their best to market their products or services while spending time with people they like and trust. A light bulb lit up in my head, and I started building relationships, both business and personal. Some of the members became my friends, and are to this day even if they're not in the group any more.

After a couple of years, somebody asked me if I would consider being president. After thinking about it for a little while, I thought I might give it a try. So I became the group's leader and have served off and on as president ever since.

It's still sometimes a little bit hard to go to networking events that will be full of mostly strangers, but it has gotten easier. One strategy I've been trying is to go with acquaintances. It makes it less intimidating to know I have friends there. It's also a great ice-breaker to introduce your friend to somebody else at the gathering, and promote your friend's business.

Another thing I try to do is go over and talk to the person in the corner, the one who can't seem to gather up enough courage to introduce herself around. I was once that person in the corner, and I always appreciated it when somebody went out of their way to be friendly to me.

I'd like to say a word about Your Networking Universe. It was founded in Denver by a guy named Mark Hiatt, who subsequently moved to Arizona and then to Portland and started chapters in each location. Then he changed the name from Colorado Business Leads to Business Leads of America, and finally to Your Networking Universe.

Mark's theory of networking is different from many other referral groups. Some of these focus almost solely on referrals, and members may be fined if they don't bring a lead to every single meeting. This inevitably results in a lot of garbage leads.

Mark believes, and I completely agree with him, that referrals follow relationships. People do business with people they know, like and trust. So our focus is not specifically on referrals, but on activities that help build relationships: one-on-ones and rapport-building events such as our annual holiday party and summer bowling parties. Members also get credit for group-building actions such as inviting guests to a meeting and introducing members to power partners.

Power partners, by the way, are businesspeople who seek the same customers as you but don't compete directly. Realtors, for instance, have many potential power partners: mortgage loan officers, bankers, service providers such as painters, carpenters, house cleaners and handymen, home inspectors and on and on.

I find such incredible support in my networking groups (I've since helped start two more YNU groups). I really feel like my fellow group members are my extended family.

Having been a dedicated networker for nearly 15 years, I've discovered that it has improved me tremendously. I'm a much more confident person, and my skills, both business and personal, have gotten better as a result.

Strangely enough, my experience with my ex-husband has made me better too. Whatever doesn't kill you makes you stronger, the proverb goes, and that has definitely been true for me.

When you come out the other side from a bad experience, you get to the point where some things aren't as important as others. Coming out of my marriage, I was done with being taken advantage of and treated like crap.

To cite just one example: Early in my real estate career, I presented an offer from my buyer client to a listing agent.

He picked my offer apart, and even worse, treated me like an idiot. I sort of cowered and took it. Today I wouldn't put up with being treated like that.

But back to networking. There's another advantage that only became evident to me after awhile. Networking can help you be a connector.

Here's what I mean by being a connector.

Everybody needs services at one time or another, and for many people, the problem is how to identify competent and honest providers who'll do a good job for them at a fair price.

There are many services that attempt to connect consumers to providers.

The problem is that most of these are pay to play—that is, to get on the list you kick in a fee, and you may not even have to be any good. So consumers using these services can't really be confident of what they'll be getting.

A much better way to identify, say, a plumber or an electrician or a carpenter is to use one recommended by someone who knows the level of service the contractor will provide.

Someone like ... hmm ... me, who meets hundreds of providers through my daily business activities and my networking.

I love love love to help people, and one of the best ways I can do this is by being a resource. I have a database of hundreds of providers who I recommend. For every one of these providers, I've either personally used their services or know someone who has. This is important to me because when I recommend a service provider to a friend, my reputation is at stake. If I recommend someone and they do a lousy job, it harms me in the eyes of the friend to whom I gave the recommendation.

I hate to hear stories about people who received rotten service, and part of my aim is to prevent this from happening to my family and friends. So I consider it an extension of my real estate service to help them find good help. Not only are you helping somebody avoid a bad experience, but you're helping a deserving business.

I pound it into my clients' heads that if they need a product or service, chances are excellent that I know somebody who can help them.

I've found that not only does this help my clients, it helps my business reputation. Realtors unfortunately are among the least-trusted professionals, and I want to do my part to dispel that image.

One word of caution: Just because somebody you know recommends a service provider doesn't necessarily mean it's because that service provider is any good. There may be business relationships that you don't know about.

For instance, a major real estate corporation recently launched an affiliated mortgage operation. I don't know what the business relationship is between the mortgage operation and the real estate agents out on the street, but it's not much of a stretch to assume that they get a commission when their clients choose that particular mortgage company based on the agent's recommendation.

Did they recommend their affiliated mortgage company because it's the best, or because of their own self-interest?

That's why I always suggest that you ask why your agent (or anybody else, for that matter) is recommending a specific service provider. Ask me, too. In my case, it's because I know that provider will do the job. If you're suspicious at all about a recommendation, ask if your agent is getting a fee from the service provider. If the answer is yes, or even if you suspect it would be yes if the agent were telling the truth, I would steer away from that provider.

Probably from that agent too.

Chapter 10
What I've Learned About Life

When I was new to real estate more than 20 years ago, there weren't too many women in the industry. The stereotypical agent at that time was a middle-aged or older man in a fancy suit driving a BMW or a Jaguar. (Earlier, the standard car for a Realtor was a Cadillac or a Lincoln–those hogs that have gone out of fashion now.)

Other agents, mostly male, treated me differently because I was a woman. I felt I needed to project a certain image.

So I dressed to the nines, drove a big car and tried to act as straight-laced as I could. I was afraid that if I didn't, I wouldn't get any business.

But as I began to have some success, I got to thinking. I didn't enjoy acting like somebody I wasn't. It put a layer of tension over my life that wasn't welcome.

So I decided to be myself, not only when I was off but when I was working. That simple change in my own mind has made all the difference.

I've never been one to desire a Beamer or a Lexus. For years, my business vehicle was a mid-sized Chrysler Sebring. It never would have done in the old days. But I was comfortable with it and my customers didn't seem to care. (And if they did care about something like that, they probably weren't anybody I wanted to work with anyway.)

So now I dress in business casual. It's comfortable for me and doesn't set me up as somebody who's above my customers.

And in 2015, I bought a car even less stereotypical for a Realtor: a cute little red VW bug. I even stuck black dots on it and put eyelashes over the headlights so that it looked like a ladybug. You can't believe how cute it is!

I love driving it and seeing people react when I go by.

I think we all need a little bit more humor in our lives. The bug perfectly matches my personality: whimsical and not too serious.

(While my car may make me seem laid back and not confrontational, you can be assured that when it comes to serving my clients, I'm not as nice as I look!)

One day recently I got a call from a buyer who had seen my sign in front of one of my listings. I drove the bug to the house, where I met her.

I was somewhat concerned that she would be put off by the VW. Then she started telling me how she had visited with a mortgage lender to get prequalified for a loan, and how he was one of those all-business guys: stark and not that friendly. She didn't care for that style of doing business.

So when she saw me get out of the bug, she was relieved because she knew working with me would be a more relaxing experience.

Another lesson I've taken to heart goes back to my first marriage. I took his abuse for many years because I'm basically a non-confrontational person.

But finally getting out of that marriage had all kinds of good effects on me. Finally standing up for myself felt incredible. Almost overnight I got stronger. And now I'm never afraid to stick up for myself and especially for my clients.

While I don't go out of my way to start a confrontation, I won't let anybody take advantage of me. It's like the old saying goes: I didn't start a fight, but if you choose to start one, I'll finish it.

I feel incredibly lucky that I've been able to do what I love every day. I love my job and I feel privileged that I'm able to make a living at it.

I've learned that you can't be all things to all people, so the only thing to do is just be yourself. Sure, you're not going to click with some people, but that's OK. It's too exhausting pretending to be somebody you're not.

Be true to yourself and the universe will take care of you. I truly believe this.

www.ingramcontent.com/pod-product-compliance
Lightning Source LLC
Chambersburg PA
CBHW071420220526
45469CB00004B/1352